FASHION ILLUSTRATION

ALL COLOUR PAPERBACKS
Other titles include

Erté
Mucha
Alma Tadema
Burne-Jones
Kate Greenaway
The Orientalists
The Liberty Style
Tiffany
Poiret

BEER 1921. 'Chloë', an evening gown illustrated by Siméon in *Gazette du Bon Ton*.

FASHION ILLUSTRATION

A RIZZOLI PAPERBACK

Rizzoli
NEW YORK

PICTURE SOURCE
All illustrations are from the archives of Academy Editions.

First published in the United States of America in 1979 by
RIZZOLI INTERNATIONAL PUBLICATIONS, INC.
712 Fifth Avenue/New York 10019

Library of Congress Catalog Card Number 79-64758
ISBN 0-8478-0248-5

Printed and bound in Hong Kong

INTRODUCTION

Throughout the 19th century, the engraved plate had become an increasingly important aspect of fashion journalism, aimed primarily at the home dressmaker eager to copy the latest styles. Usually produced by teams of anonymous artists, each one dealing with a different part of the design, the genre had fossilized into a stereotyped shorthand of insipid faces and stilted poses, overburdened by a mass of detail showing the construction and trimming of each garment. The average fashion plate was useful but uninspired, and was in grave danger of being superseded by the photograph. By the early years of the 20th century, the standard of photographic reproduction had improved sufficiently to encourage at least one leading French magazine, *Les Modes,* to depend entirely on photographs, mostly half-tone but with a few tipped-in colour plates. Aesthetically, these were scarcely more exciting than the engravings they replaced, but they had at least the advantage of conveying a sense of actuality.

In 1908, however, something happened to change all this. A young Parisian couturier with a genius for self-advertisement commissioned an unknown artist to produce a small album of fashion illustrations. *Les Robes de Paul Poiret* by Paul Iribe inaugurated a period of fruitful collaboration between artists and designers, an era in the history of fashion illustration which has never been equalled.

Poiret's originality lay in his understanding that the couturier is in the business of selling dreams as well as clothes, and that realism is almost always inimical to this process. By allowing free scope to one artist's graphic fantasy, he could convey a far more potent message.

Iribe's drawings were crisp and economical (Plate 1). Backgrounds were minimal and monochromatic, consisting of a piece of furniture, a picture on the wall or a balustrade, just enough to suggest a shallow stage-like space. All the emphasis was concentrated on the dresses, blocks of flat unmodulated colour with a bare minimum of detail. The album as a whole was stylish, witty and above all, modern, thoroughly in keeping with the radical simplicity of the clothes themselves.

Fashion was moving away from the extravagant corseted curves of the Edwardian silhouette towards a softer and more natural line. The dresses of 1908 were narrow and high-waisted with details like tiny ruffs and frogged fastenings, testifying to an overt revival of the Directoire fashions of the 1790s. Indeed, an element of fancy-dress was to characterise the period as a whole.

In 1911, the Iribe book was followed by an equally lavish album, *Les Choses de Paul Poiret,* by Georges Lepape. Clearly these occasional productions could not provide a sufficiently regular showcase for fashion illustration to develop as a genre, but their success inspired the launching, in 1912, of several de luxe magazines, *Modes et Manières d'Aujourd'hui, Journal des Dames et des Modes* and the *Gazette du Bon Ton.* Like their predecessors, all the illustrations were printed by the *pochoir* method, a laborious process in which the design was built up with numerous metal stencils, each coloured in by hand using gouache paint. It was a time-consuming and expensive process, but it preserved the liveliness of the original drawing in a way that mechanical means could not, and, after all, exclusive luxury was part of the appeal of these magazines. The *Gazette du Bon Ton* spoke for them all when it announced its intention to be 'a showcase in which only the most luxurious examples of high fashion and the best of the decorative arts could be displayed, regardless of the cost involved.'

The most consistently good of the many limited edition magazines which appeared during the next few years was probably the *Gazette du Bon Ton.* Its *directeur,* Lucien Vogel, assembled a team of regular illustrators, the best known of whom included Paul Iribe, Georges Lepape, Charles Martin, Etienne Drian, George Barbier, André Marty, Robert Bonfils and Pierre Mourgue. Vogel gave his artists *carte blanche* to interpret the fashions in their own way and each developed a distinctive style (although one common theme was the use of witty or allusive titles to suggest a story behind each picture).

As we have seen, there was no tradition of good fashion illustration to draw upon, but this proved to be an advantage, encouraging these artists to look to the other visual arts for inspiration. They were very conscious of their links with avant-garde painting, with its tendency towards a more decorative use of flatness and non-naturalistic colour; while within the graphic arts, posters and illustrated books had been enjoying a renaissance since the 1890s. From such diverse artists as Lautrec and Beardsley, Gauguin and Matisse, the illustrators learned how to deploy their figures within a brilliantly coloured setting, without compromising the essential flatness of the page.

But perhaps the greatest stimulus of all was provided by non-European sources, in particular the jewel-like quality of Persian and Indian miniatures (Plate 5) and the elegant simplicity of 18th century Japanese prints.

Not only the illustrators but the whole fashionable world was in love with the East. 1908, the year of the Iribe album, also witnessed the eruption of the Ballets Russes onto the Paris stage. Under the inspired direction of Diaghilev, the Russian ballet was probably the single most important influence on the decorative arts of the period. In particular the 1910 production of Scheherezade, designed by Léon Bakst, encouraged a vogue for exotic, oriental styles which lasted well into the 20s.

If she was exotic and sophisticated by night, in the elegant creations of designers such as Worth and Beer, by day the fashionable Parisienne did her best to look demure (Plates 8 and 9) after the manner of Kate Greenaway. The rather ambivalent appeal of this image had much in common with the success, a few years earlier, of Colette's Claudine novels and their salaciously innocent schoolgirl heroine.

This night-and-day polarisation of the feminine image was by no means new, of course. The dual fantasy of Madonna/Eve, or the virgin and the vamp, had been one of the most potent images of *fin-de-siècle* symbolism, and was brought up to date by those heroines of the silent cinema, 'good' wholesome Mary Pickford and 'bad' seductive Theda Bara.

The broad outlines of fashionable dress up to 1914 changed very little from the slender high-waisted tube established by Poiret. Occasionally a broadbrimmed hat would be used to balance this narrow silhouette (Plate 2) but the trend was towards much smaller, neater heads. This move, prefigured by the bandeaux in Iribe's 1908 drawings, was epitomised by the turban (Plates 3, 4 and 7). This innovation was inspired, according to Poiret, by the sight of the girls who worked in his salon tying pieces of brightly coloured fabric around their heads to protect their hair, although the success of the style was due mainly to its oriental associations.

The mainstays of the couture trade continued to be the elegant tea gown and the evening dress, but the pressure of changing social customs was beginning to be felt. As can be seen from Paquin's design in Plate 6, the tailored suit, once associated principally with the militant 'New Woman' of the 1890s, was becoming softer and more acceptable. Fashionable sports made new demands (Plate 7) while the agility needed to negotiate the tango and the foxtrot encouraged a trend towards fuller, shorter skirts, largely brought about by the evolution of the tunic. Originally introduced as an Arabian Nights fantasy, it created a layered effect, breaking up the elongated proportions of the earlier Empire line and shifting attention down from the high waist (Plates 8 and 11). The same result was sometimes achieved by embroidered panels or changes of colour (Plates 9 and 10). By the eve of war, this overskirt had dropped to just above the ankle, carrying the main line of the garment and making the underdress virtually redundant, as in Doeuillet's summer dress (Plate 12).

The effect of the First World War on fashion was at first confined to the material shortages it entailed; the physical and psychological damage inflicted on society would take longer to manifest itself. Reduced paper supplies caused many magazines to close down or to appear only sporadically in a truncated form. There was a shortage of the heavier fabrics, needed for the troops, while the northern textile manufacturing areas were soon under enemy occupation.

Despite these problems the fashion industry was not seen as a frivolous diversion but as an important contribution to the civilian war effort - both for the economic value of its exports and as a bulwark of French civilisation. French women were exhorted, as their patriotic duty, to look as feminine and elegant as possible, to boost the morale of the soldiers on leave; while in 1915 a joint French/American edition of the *Gazette du Bon Ton* trumpeted, 'since the Latin races are fighting to uphold their taste against Teutonic barbarity was it not to be expected that Paris fashion should once again take the lead this spring?'

How far the war accelerated the trend towards shorter skirts is difficult to define. Unlike the raising of hemlines during the Second World War, there was no saving on materials, since the shorter styles acquired a compensating increase in width. Greater mobility was undoubtedly a factor, but the more active role demanded of many women scarcely impinged upon the lives of the fashionable clients of the *grands couturiers,* whose war work was more likely to centre round the charity bazaar than the munitions factory.

As usual, fashion's response to social and political change worked on a more subtle level of visual symbolism, crystallising the mood and aspirations of the time. The fashionable Parisienne of the war years wanted to look dashing and rather gallant, and her femininity was enhanced rather than compromised by 'military' detailing and rakish, upswept hats. The quiescent vertical lines of the pre-war silhouette were replaced by more active diagonals - flaring skirts and upturned 'Medici' collars. For evening, the mood was softer but with a distinctly modern air of transatlantic sophistication, exemplified in an early drawing by Erté (Plate 13).

The period immediately following the Armistice was characterised by a mood of instability, as society tried uneasily to come to terms with the grotesque implications of four years of carnage. Dada painters and poets glorified irrationality, questioning the cultural values of the generation which had led them into war, and proclaiming the futility of art. At the other extreme, Jean Cocteau issued his 'rappel à l'ordre' - a call for a return to classical values in art, a mood reflected in the decorative arts by an enormous interest in 18th century themes, as if artists were trying to recapture a golden age in French cultural history.

Fashion design shared this loss of equilibrium. Skirts were the main focus of interest, often accentuated by a differently coloured bodice (Plates 20 and 21). They rose and fell, flared, ballooned and subsided again, before finally settling on the low-waisted tubular shape that was to characterise the decade.

Publication of the de luxe magazines had by now resumed, augmented in 1919 by La Guirlande and Les Feuillets d'Art, and in 1920 by Art, Goût, Beauté and by a host of single albums.

The illustrators proved surprisingly adaptable to the changed mood. Even Georges Lepape, whose confidently graceful line had epitomised the pre-war period, adopted a much sketchier style, incorporating quasi-cubist distortions and discontinuities (Plate 17) while the oldest member of the pre-war Gazette group, Charles Martin, who was 70 in 1918, found his wittily eccentric drawings (Plate 20) thoroughly attuned to the younger generation's taste for angularity.

Colours, too, were more discordant - 'daring' combinations of scarlet and cerise, acid greens and sulphurous yellows, all set off by large quantities of black.

Exotic influences were still a major theme, dominated by the discovery in 1922 of Tutankhamun's tomb, an event which sparked off a rage for Egyptian motifs and encouraged the taste for fringes and heavy kohl-rimmed eyes (Plate 26).

By day, however, the mood was essentially sporting. Skirts were getting shorter (although they would not rise above the knee until 1927, and then only for a few seasons), and the boyish 'flapper', flat-chested and short-haired, wore her clothes with the kind of casual, understated chic typified by Chanel.

Considerable ingenuity was required to combine freedom of movement with this pared down silhouette. Madeleine Vionnet's mastery of the bias cut was unequalled, but a more typical solution was the use of pleated side panels, which had the added advantage of emphasising the vertical, geometric lines of the clothes.

Since straightforward opulence was out of vogue, subtleties of cut and line - qualities which cannot be copied cheaply - were becoming an increasingly important weapon if haute couture were to maintain its edge over the expanding ready-to-wear market.

Perhaps because of this, illustrators began to place more emphasis on detail, at the expense of an overall liveliness. Certainly the quality of fashion illustration was beginning to decline by the middle of the decade, with photography starting to take over again. Economic factors played a part in this process - the age of the luxury hand-printed edition was over.

When the Gazette du Bon Ton was forced to close in 1925, only Art, Goût, Beauté continued to produce hand-coloured illustrations. And though the girls who saunter through the pages of Art, Goût, Beauté playing their endless games of golf are quite delightful, their current appeal depends on a nostalgic period charm.

Their fate should not surprise us. Fashion is, after all, the most time-bound of the arts. But the achievement of the heroic years of the de luxe magazines had been to turn fashion illustrations into minor works of art, so complete within themselves that they could defy time.

Pauline Ridley

1

POIRET
1908
Three gowns.
Paul Iribe
Les Robes de Paul Poiret

2

1912
Pleated white lawn blouse
worn under a slender black satin dress.
J. Gojé
Journal des Dames et des Modes

3

1912
Embroidered white crêpe dress
worn under a green velvet blouse
with designs woven in red.
Charles Martin
Journal des Dames et des Modes

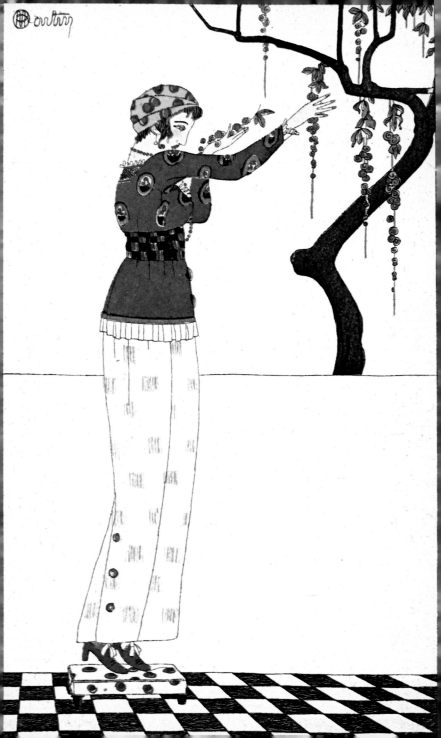

4

1912
'Pénélope'
House coat of crêpe de Chine with
co-ordinating jacket trimmed with flowers.
Georges Lepape
Gazette du Bon Ton

Georges Lepape

5

REDFERN
1913
'De la Pomme aux Lèvres'
Fancy dress of brush velvet bespangled with
silver, revealing a chiffon undergarment.
Charles Martin
Gazette du Bon Ton

6

PAQUIN
1913
'Au Jardin des Hespérides'
Suit of black and white chequered
cloth trimmed with black satin.
George Barbier
Gazette du Bon Ton

G. BARBIER 1913

7

1913
'Pour St. Moritz'
Suit of white rateen, embroidered in
wool and trimmed with skunk fur.
George Barbier
Journal des Dames et des Modes

G. BARBIER 1913

8

1913
'La Belle et la Bête'
Silk housecoat under a printed crêpe de
Chine jacket trimmed with a large frill.
Charles Martin
Gazette du Bon Ton

9

PAQUIN
1913
'Un Peu . . .'
Country dress of white crêpe with blue
embroidery.
George Barbier
Gazette du Bon Ton

10

REDFERN
1913
'Sur la Falaise'
Summer dress of red and white silk
tulle with a coral buckle at the waist.
J. Gojé
Gazette du Bon Ton

11

PAQUIN
1913
'Le Jeu des Grâces'
Spotted silk dress; the bodice trimmed with
velvet reveals a white tulle blouse and
layered tunic.
George Barbier
Gazette du Bon Ton

12

DOEUILLET
1914
'Le Cyprès et la Rose'
Embroidered tulle summer dress caught in at
the waist by a pink crêpe de Chine belt.
George Barbier
Gazette du Bon Ton

13

ERTE
1915
Evening dress with green taffeta
top and embroidered skirt and shawl.

14

JENNY
1919
Silver lamé evening gown with full pale
blue chiffon skirt and belt of pink roses.
Umberto Brunelleschi
La Guirlande

15

BARCLAY
1919
Evening gown of mauve silk and pale chiffon.
Umberto Brunelleschi
La Guirlande

16

WORTH
1920
Silver lamé evening gown with long flowing
train, the folds gathered up and secured by a
pearl brooch.
Bernard Boutet de Monvel
Gazette du Bon Ton

17

POIRET
1920
'La Belle Journée'
Muslin dress printed in pink and
black with organdi collar and sleeves.
Georges Lepape
Gazette du Bon Ton

18

1920
Yellow organdi dress and muslin cape with
jade green lining and black velvet ribbons.
Robert Bonfils
Le Goût du Jour

19

DOBBS
1920
Advertisement for a suit.
Emmanuel Blanche
La Guirlande

E BLANCHE

20

RODIER
1920
'Et Puis Voici Mon Coeur . . .'
Summer dress of Ceylon voile with
chequered blue crêpe bodice.
Charles Martin
Gazette du Bon Ton

21

1920
'Les Fleurs du Voisin'
Garden party dress of organdi and taffeta in
the style of Louis XVI. The collar and panels
are trimmed with delicate white embroidery.
Robert Bonfils
Gazette du Bon Ton

22

WORTH
1920
'La Femme à l'Eventail'
Silver and green damask evening gown
trimmed with silver lace.
Etienne Drian
Gazette du Bon Ton

23

WORTH
1921
'Jota'
Yellow crêpe de Chine evening coat
with white embroidery and fringes.
Edouard Benito
Gazette du Bon Ton

24

RODIER
1921
'Adieu, Pauvre Amour . . .'
Afternoon dress of black satin and
'Palmes Agnella', a Rodier fabric.
Georges Lepape
Gazette du Bon Ton

25

1921
'La Promenade du Palais-Royal'
Woollen redingote with organdi tie.
Pierre Mourgue
Gazette du Bon Ton

Mourgue.
21.

26

WORTH
1921
'La Belle Dame sans Merci'
Crêpe evening gown worn over a silk tunic.
George Barbier
Gazette du Bon Ton

GEORGE BARBIER 1921

27

RODIER
1922
'Suzanne et le Pacifique'
Beach dress in a woollen fabric,
'Chevrons Laine'.
Siméon
Gazette du Bon Ton

28

BEER
1922
'Sortilèges'
Evening gown with silver chiffon bodice
embroidered with diamonds and skirt of
tinted pearls over silver lace.
George Barbier
Gazette du Bon Ton

29

ROGER
1922
'Les Cinq Sens: 1. - L'Odorat'
Black velvet hats with ostrich feathers.
Pierre Mourgue
Gazette du Bon Ton

30

VIONNET
1922
Dress.
Thayaht
Gazette du Bon Ton

31

POIRET
1922
'En Plein Coeur'
Evening dress of black velvet and green
crêpe de Chine with jet embroidery.
André Marty
Gazette du Bon Ton

32

WORTH
1922
'La Roseraie'
Crêpe evening gown with train
attached by a golden rose.
George Barbier
Gazette du Bon Ton

33

LANVIN
1922
'Le Nid de Pinsons'
Burgundy dress with a belt of fabric flowers
and tulle bodice trimmed with burgundy
ruching.
André Marty
Gazette du Bon Ton

34

1923
DOEUILLET
'Loulou'
Three-piece dress of crêpe du Maroc
embroidered with red leather and silver
thread.
PREMET
'Handicap'
White crêpe dress with a belt of printed silk.
Art, Goût, Beauté

Art - Goût - Beauté

35

VIONNET
1923
'Automnale'
Suit.
Thayaht
Gazette du Bon Ton

36

LANVIN
1923
'La Présentation du Miroir'
Green and white evening gown trimmed
with ribbons and lace.
Georges Lepape
Gazette du Bon Ton

37

MOLYNEUX
1924
'Le Golf à Cagnes'
White jersey three-piece trimmed with beaver.
Art, Goût, Beauté

Art - Goût - Beauté

38

PATOU
1924
'Le Village de Luceram'
Casual dress of white crêpe du Maroc with a
multicoloured flower printed jacket.
Art, Goût, Beauté

39

1924
DRECOLL
'Géo'
Multicoloured organdi dress with abstract
designs.
MADELEINE
'Rose Pompon'
Mauve and pink organdi dress decorated
with flowers.
Art, Goût, Beauté

40

LANVIN
1924
'Le Rouleau de Musique'
Pale blue afternoon dress with
silver and gold braiding.
Georges Lepape
Gazette du Bon Ton

41

1924
MARTIAL ET ARMAND
'Printanière'
White cotton dress embroidered with
coloured motifs.
PHILIPPE ET GASTON
'Andrinople'
White crêpe de Chine three-piece with
borders and jacket of printed cloth.
Art, Goût, Beauté

42

1924
MOLYNEUX
Short velvet cape with honeycomb design.
MARTIAL ET ARMAND
'Marmaille'
Green crêpe du Maroc dress trimmed with
embroidered black crêpe.
'Pochette'
Red ottoman dress embroidered with gold
thread.
Art, Goût, Beauté

43

MARTIAL ET ARMAND
1925
Black ottoman three-piece
trimmed with braid.
Art, Goût, Beauté

44

1925
MARTIAL ET ARMAND
'Bécassine'
Dress suit of blue rep
trimmed with red leather.
DRECOLL
'Nerzo'
Afternoon coat of black wool
with tartan trim.
Art, Goût, Beauté

45

DOUCET
1925
'Fugitive'
Black lace dress trimmed with diamonds.
Art, Goût, Beauté

46

1925
LELONG
'Adieu Petit'
Violet crêpe dress trimmed with red ribbons.
POIRET
'Chaumière'
Royal blue cotton voile dress with
white embroidery and white voile flounces.
Art, Goût, Beauté

47

DOEUILLET
1925
'Flafla'
Brightly coloured printed muslin dress.
Art, Goût, Beauté

48

1925
POIRET
Brown and white crêpe de Chine
dress trimmed with leather.
DOUCET
'Leda'
Mauve crêpe dress with a black feather belt.
Art, Goût, Beauté